COTTONMOUTHS

THE SNAKE DISCOVERY LIBRARY

Sherie Bargar, 1944 Linda Johnson

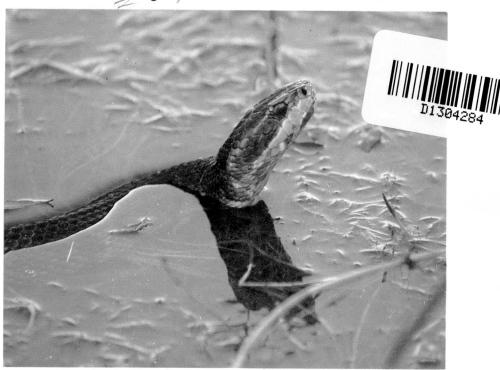

Photographer/Consultant: George Van Horn

Rourke Publishing Group
Vero Beach, Florida 32964

Library of Congress Cataloging in Publication Data

Bargar, Sherie, 1944-
   Cottonmouths.

   (The Snake discovery library)
   Summary: An introduction to the physical
characteristics, habits, natural environment,
and relationship to human beings of various species
of cottonmouths, also known as water moccasins.
   1. Agkistrodon piscivorus—Juvenile literature.
2. Pit-vipers—Juvenile literature.   3. Poisonous
snakes—Juvenile literature.   [1. Water moccasin.
2. Poisonous snakes. 3. Snakes] I. Johnson,
Linda, 1947-   . II. Title. III. Series:
Bargar, Sherie, 1944-   . Snake discovery library.
QL666.069B374   1986   597.96   86-15553
ISBN 0-86592-958-0

TABLE OF CONTENTS

COTTONMOUTHS

Cottonmouths are relatives of rattlesnakes and other poisonous pit vipers in the *Crotalid* family. Unlike most of their relatives, they prefer to live and hunt in fresh water **habitats**. They are known as Cottonmouths because of the white linings of their mouths. Cottonmouths have been known to live over 20 years.

ottonmouth
Agkistrodon piscivorous

WHERE THEY LIVE

Swamps, lakes, rivers, and marshlands of the southeastern United States are the homes of Cottonmouths. They often **bask** at the water's edge. When wetlands and ponds dry up, hungry Cottonmouths will travel great distances to be near water. This **migration** may lead hundreds of Cottonmouths to one small pond in search of **prey** and a suitable **habitat**.

Cottonmouth
Agkistrodon piscivorou

HOW THEY LOOK

The heavy-bodied Cottonmouth may be 4 to 5 feet long. The olive, brown, and black scales have ridges and **pores** on them. Some have bands which are dark brown with a light color on each side of them, and some Cottonmouths become a solid dark color. The Cottonmouth seems to be wearing a mask because a dark band runs from each eye to the corner of its mouth.

ottonmouth
Agkistrodon piscivorous

THEIR SENSES

The Cottonmouth's tongue flicks out and brings in particles from the surrounding area. The Jacobson's organ in the roof of its mouth **analyzes** the particles to learn what is nearby. The sense of smell is helped by the senses of sight and heat. At close range the Cottonmouth uses its sight to locate moving **prey**. The heat receptor pits on the face sense the warmth of **prey**.

Cottonmouth
Agkistrodon piscivorous

THE HEAD AND MOUTH

The Cottonmouth's big, chunky head has a flat top. Long, hollow fangs are folded against the roof of its mouth. During the bite the fangs are extended to inject **venom** from the venom gland into the **prey**. The jaws stretch like a rubber band to swallow animals whole. The windpipe extends from the throat to the front of the mouth and lets the snake breathe while swallowing **prey**.

Cottonmouth
Agkistrodon piscivorou

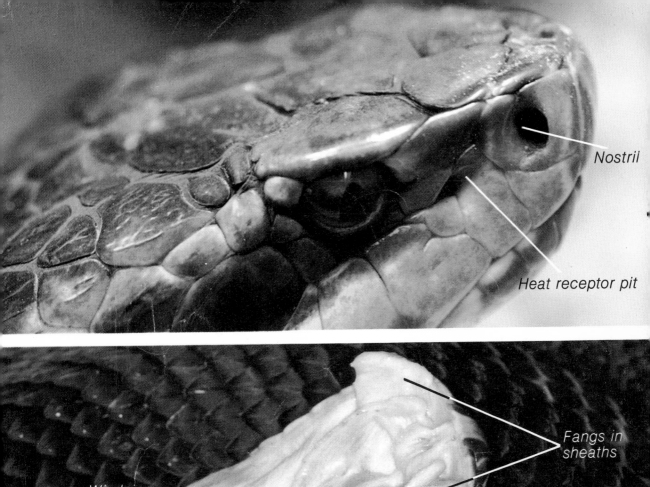

Nostril

Heat receptor pit

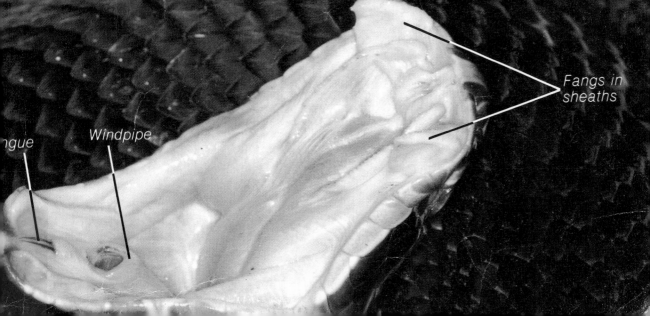

Fangs in
sheaths

ngue

Windpipe

BABY COTTONMOUTHS

In August or September a mother Cottonmouth has 5 to 15 babies. The babies are about 10 inches long. At birth, the baby Cottonmouth has bright patterns with bands and a brillant yellow tail. As it grows older, the bright pattern fades, and the snake becomes darker. The baby Cottonmouth wiggles its tail to attract **prey**. The bite of the Cottonmouth can kill small **prey** the minute it is born.

Cottonmouth
Agkistrodon piscivorou

PREY

Cottonmouths are good swimmers who often hunt for **prey** in water. Fish, frogs, birds, ducks, small turtles, and other small animals are their **prey**. The Cottonmouth also eats other snakes. The Cottonmouth surprises its **prey** with a quick, **poisonous** bite and swallows it immediately. Alligators, birds, and raccoons eat the Cottonmouth.

ttonmouth
Agkistrodon piscivorous

THEIR DEFENSES

The Cottonmouth avoids an enemy whenever it can. If escape is impossible, the Cottonmouth stands its ground by showing its fangs and the white lining of its mouth. Shaking its tail, the snake warns the enemy that it is in danger. If the enemy comes too close, the Cottonmouth strikes.

Cottonmouth
Agkistrodon piscivorou

COTTONMOUTHS AND PEOPLE

Because of its poor eyesight, the Cottonmouth often enters a fisherman's boat. Unaware of the fisherman, the shy Cottonmouth is attracted to the smell of fish or looking for a place to rest. It is not attacking the fisherman even though it may look like it. Trying to enter water to escape a hunter, the Cottonmouth may seem to attack by rushing near or through the hunter's legs.

The bite of the Cottonmouth is painful. It causes swelling and damages the tissue around the bite.

GLOSSARY

analyze (AN a lyze) analyzes — To find out what something is.

bask (BASK) — To lie in and enjoy warmth.

habitat (HAB i tat) habitats — A place where an animal is usually found.

migration (MI gra tion) — To travel from one place to another.

poison (POI son) poisonous — A substance that causes sickness or death when it enters the body.

pore (PORE) pores — A tiny hole.

prey (PREY) — An animal hunted or killed by another animal for food.

venom (VEN om) — A chemical made in animals that makes other animals and people sick or kills them.

INDEX